The Cat
and the
Moon

and
Other
Cat Poems

THE BRITISH LIBRARY

First published in 2014 by
The British Library
96 Euston Road
London NW1 2DB

ISBN 978 0 7123 5747 0

The following poems are reproduced by kind permission of the copyright holders:

'Five Eyes' copyright © The Literary Trustees of Walter de la Mare and the Society of Authors as their representation; 'The Year-Old Kitten' by permission of the James Kirkup Collection; 'Mr Sheraton's Cat' and 'To Coney: My Kitten' from *Blackbird Has Spoken* by Eleanor Farjeon (published by Macmillan) courtesy of David Higham; 'The Story of Kruger the Cat' and 'I Had a Little Cat' from *I Had a Little Cat: Collected Poems for Children* by Charles Causley (published by Macmillan) courtesy of David Higham; 'This Old Cat' copyright © K.C. Sievert Bingamon (for Misty-Dawn, 1998).

British Library Cataloguing in Publication Data
A catalogue record for this book is available from the British Library

Designed and typeset in Perpetua by illuminati, Grosmont
Printed and bound in Hong Kong by Great Wall Printing Co. Ltd

The Cat and the Moon
WILLIAM BUTLER YEATS (1865–1939)

The cat went here and there
And the moon spun round like a top,
And the nearest kin of the moon,
The creeping cat, looked up.
Black Minnaloushe stared at the moon,
For, wander and wail as he would,
The pure cold light in the sky
Troubled his animal blood.
Minnaloushe runs in the grass
Lifting his delicate feet.
Do you dance, Minnaloushe, do you dance?
When two close kindred meet.
What better than call a dance?
Maybe the moon may learn,
Tired of that courtly fashion,
A new dance turn.
Minnaloushe creeps through the grass
From moonlit place to place,
The sacred moon overhead
Has taken a new phase.
Does Minnaloushe know that his pupils
Will pass from change to change,
And that from round to crescent,

From crescent to round they range?
Minnaloushe creeps through the grass
Alone, important and wise,
And lifts to the changing moon
His changing eyes.

From The Wild Swans at Coole

Kitty: What She Thinks of Herself
WILLIAM BRIGHTY RANDS (1823–1882)

I am the cat of cats. I am
The everlasting cat!
Cunning, and old, and sleek as jam,
The everlasting cat!
I hunt vermin in the night –
The everlasting cat!
For I see best without the light –
The everlasting cat!

She Sights a Bird — She Chuckles

EMILY DICKINSON (1830–1886)

She sights a Bird — she chuckles —
She flattens — then she crawls —
She runs without the look of feet —
Her eyes increase to Balls —

Her Jaws stir — twitching — hungry —
Her Teeth can hardly stand —
She leaps, but Robin leaped the first —
Ah, Pussy, of the Sand,

The Hopes so juicy ripening —
You almost bathed your Tongue —
When Bliss disclosed a hundred Toes —
And fled with every one —

Five Eyes

WALTER DE LA MARE (1873–1956)

In Hans' old Mill his three black cats
Watch the bins for the thieving rats.
Whisker and claw, they crouch in the night,
Their five eyes smouldering green and bright:
Squeaks from the flour sacks, squeaks from where
The cold wind stirs on the empty stair,
Squeaking and scampering, everywhere.
Then down they pounce, now in, now out,
At whisking tail, and sniffing snout;
While lean old Hans he snores away
Till peep of light at break of day;
Then up he climbs to his creaking mill,
Out come his cats all grey with meal –
Jekkel, and Jessup, and one-eyed Jill.

The Cat
W.H. DAVIES (1871–1940)

Within that porch, across the way,
I see two naked eyes this night;
Two eyes that neither shut nor blink,
Searching my face with a green light.

But cats to me are strange, so strange –
I cannot sleep if one is near;
And though I'm sure I see those eyes
I'm not so sure a body's there!

A Cat
ROBERT HERRICK (1591–1674)

A Cat
I keep, that plays about my House.
Grown fat
With eating many a minching Mouse.

Marigold
RICHARD GARNETT (1835–1906)

She moved through the garden in glory because
She had very long claws at the end of her paws.
Her back was arched, her tail was high.
A green fire glared in her vivid eye;
And all the toms, though never so bold,
Quailed at the martial Marigold.

From *The Cats' Newspaper* (c. 1808)

Grimalkin
JOHN PHILIPS (1676–1709)

Grimalkin to Domestick Vermin sworn
An everlasting Foe, with watchful Eye
Lies nightly brooding o'er a chinky Gap
Protending her fell Claws, to thoughtless Mice
Sure Ruin.

The Cat of the House
FORD MADOX FORD (1873–1939)

I muse
Over the hearth with my 'minishing eyes
Until after
The last coal dies.
Every tunnel of the mouse,
Every channel of the cricket,
I have smelt,
I have felt
The secret shifting of the mouldered rafter,
And heard
Every bird in the thicket.
I see
You
Nightingale up in the tree!...
I born of a race of strange things,
Of deserts, great temples, great kings,
In the hot sands where the nightingale never sings!

One o'Clock
KATHERINE LYLE (1863–1938)

One of the Clock, and silence deep,
Then up the Stairway, black and steep,
The old House-Cat comes creepy-creep,
With soft feet goes from room to room,
Her green eyes shining through the gloom,
And finds all fast asleep.

From *A Fable of the Widow and Her Cat*
JONATHAN SWIFT (1667–1745)

A widow kept a favourite cat.
    At first a gentle creature;
But when he was grown sleek and fat,
With many a mouse, and many a rat
    He soon disclosed his nature.

The fox and he were friends of old,
    Nor could they now be parted;
They nightly flock to rob the fold,
Devour'd the lambs, the fleeces sold,
    And puss grew lion-hearted.

He scratched her maid, he stole the cream,
    He tore her best lace pinner;
Nor Chanticleer upon the beam,
Nor chick, nor duckling, 'scapes when Grim
    Invites the fox to dinner.

The dame full wisely did decree,
    For fear he should dispatch more,
That the false wretch should worried be:
But in a saucy manner he
    Thus speeched it like a Lechmere.

'Must I, against all right and law,
    Like pole-cat vile be treated?
I! who so long with tooth and claw
Have kept domestic mice in awe
    And foreign foes defeated!'

'Your golden pippins, and your pies,
    How oft have I defended?
'Tis true, the pinner which you prize
I tore in frolic; to your eyes
    I never harm intended.'

The Cat and the Bird
GEORGE CANNING (1770—1827)

Tell me, tell me, gentle Robin,
What is it sets thy heart a-throbbing?
Is it that Grimalkin fell
Hath killed thy father or thy mother,
Thy sister or thy brother,
Or any other?
Tell me but that,
And I'll kill the Cat.
But stay, little Robin, did you ever spare
A grub on the ground or a fly in the air?
No, that you never did, I'll swear;
So I won't kill the Cat,
That's flat.

The Lover

GEORGE TURBEVILLE (*c.* 1544—*c.* 1597)

If I might alter kinde,
    what think you I would bee?
Nor Fish, nor Foule, nor Fle nor Frog,
    nor Squirril on the tree.

The Fish the hooke, the Foule
    the lymed twig doth catch,
The Fle the Finger, and the Frog
    the Bustard doth dispatch.

The Squirril thinking nought
    that feately cracks the nut,
The greedie Goshawke wanting pray
    in dread of Death doth put.

But scorning all these kindes,
    I would become a Cat,
To combat with the creeping Mouse,
    and scratch the screecking Rat.

I would be present aye
    and at my ladies call;
To gard hir from the fearfull Mouse
    in parlour and in hall.

In kitchin for his Lyfe,
    he should not shew his head;
The Peare in Poke should lie untoucht
    when shee were gone to bed.

The Mouse should stand in feare,
    so should the squeaking Rat;
And this would I do if I were
    converted to a Cat.

The Lover, whose Mistress feared a Mouse, declareth that
he would become a Cat if he might have his Desire

From *The Manciple's Tale*
GEOFFREY CHAUCER (1343–1400)

Lat take a cat, and fostre him wel with milk,
And tendre flesh, and make his couche of silk,
And lat him seen a mous go by the wal;
Anon he weyveth milk, and flesh, and al,
And every deyntee that is in that hous,
Swich appetyt hath he to ete a mous.

From *The Canterbury Tales*

The Cat and the Rain
JONATHAN SWIFT (1667–1745)

Careful observers may foretell the hour
(By sure prognostics) when to dread a shower;
While rain depends, the pensive cat gives o'er
Her frolics, and pursues her tail no more.

Cats and Men
THOMAS FLATMAN (1637–1688)

Men ride many miles,
Cats tread many tiles,
Both hazard their necks in the fray;
    Only cats, when they fall
    From a house or a wall,
Keep their feet, mount their tails, and away!

From *An Appeal to Cats in the Business of Love*

From *Jubilate Agno*
CHRISTOPHER SMART (1722–1771)

For I will consider my Cat Jeoffry.

For he is the servant of the Living God, duly and
daily serving him...

For having done duty and received blessing he
begins to consider himself.

For this he performs in ten degrees.

For first he looks upon his forepaws to see if they
are clean.

For secondly he kicks up behind to clear away
there.

For thirdly he works it upon stretch with the
forepaws extended.

For fourthly he sharpens his paws by wood.

For fifthly he washes himself.

For sixthly he rolls upon wash.

For Seventhly he fleas himself, that he may not be
interrupted upon the beat.

For Eighthly he rubs himself against a post.

For Ninthly he looks up for his instructions.

For Tenthly he goes in quest of food...

For when his day's work is done his business more
properly begins.

For he keeps the Lord's watch in the night against
    the adversary.
For he counteracts the powers of darkness by his
    electrical skin and glaring eyes...
For in his morning orisons he loves the sun and
    the sun loves him.

The White Cat
SIR PHILIP SIDNEY (1554–1586)

I have (and long shall have) a white great nimble
    cat,
A king upon a mouse, a strong foe to the rat,
Fine eares, long taile he hath, with Lions curbed
    clawe
Which oft he lifteth up, and stayes his lifted pawe,
Deepe musing to himselfe, which after-mewing
    showes,
Till with lickt blood, his eye of fire espie his foes.

From *Second Eclogues of Arcadia*

From *The Cat*
A.C. BENSON (1862—1925)

On some grave business, soft and slow
Along the garden paths you go
   With bold and burning eyes,
Or stand with twitching tail to mark
What starts and rustles in the dark
   Among the peonies.

The dusty cockchafer that springs
Upon the dusk with shirring wings,
   The beetle glossy-horned,
The rabbit pattering through the fern
May frisk unheeded by your stern
   Preoccupation scorned.

You go, and when the morning dawns
O'er blowing trees and dewey lawns
   Dim-veiled with gossamer,
When cheery birds are on the wing,
You creep, a wild and wicked thing,
   With stained and starting fur.

You all day long beside the fire
Retrace in dreams your dark desire

And mournfully complain
In grave displeasure if I raise
Your languid form to pet or praise,
    And so to sleep again...

You loved me when the fire was warm,
But now I stretch a fondling arm,
    You eye me and depart.
Cold eye, sleek skin and velvet paws,
You win my indolent applause,
    You do not win my heart.

A Cat's Appearance
ANON

Some pussies' coats are yellow; some amber
    streaked with dark;
No member of the feline race but has a
    special mark.
This one has feet with hoarfrost tipped:
    that one has tail that curls;
Another's inky hide is striped; another's decked
    with pearls.

All Kinds of Cats
ANON

Calumnious cats, who circulate faux pas,
And reputations maul with murderous claws;
Shrill cats, whom fierce domestic brawls delight,
Cross cats, who nothing want but teeth to bite,
Starch cats of puritanic aspect sad,
And learned cats who talk their husbands mad;
Uncleanly cats who never pare their nails,
Cat-gossips, full of Canterbury tales;
Cat-grandams, vexed with asthmas and catarrhs,
And superstitious cats, who curse their stars.

Choosing their Names
THOMAS HOOD (1799—1845)

Our old cat has kittens three —
What do you think their names should be?
Pepperpot, Sootikin, Scratchaway-there,
Was there ever a kitten with these to compare?
And we call their old mother — now what do
    you think?
Tabitha Long-claws Tiddley-wink!

One is a tabby with emerald eyes,
  And a tail that's long and slender,
And into a temper she quickly flies
  If you ever by chance offend her.
    I think we shall call her this —
    I think we shall call her that —
Now, don't you think that Pepperpot
  Is a nice name for a cat?

One is black with a frill of white,
  And her feet are all white fur,
If you stroke her she carries her tail upright
  And quickly begins to purr.
    I think we shall call her this —
    I think we shall call her that —
Now, don't you think that Sootikin
  Is a nice name for a cat?

One is a tortoiseshell yellow and black,
  With plenty of white about him;
If you tease him, at once he sets up his back,
  He's a quarrelsome one, ne'er doubt him.
    I think we shall call him this —
    I think we shall call him that —
Now, don't you think that Scratchaway
  Is a nice name for a cat?

The Kitten
ANON

I sprang to life with playful, merry face
The prettiest kitten of my pretty race;
My mother purr'd her joys with fond surprise,
And watch'd with anxious care my opening eyes.

From *The Kitten in the Falling Snow*
JAMES KIRKUP (1918—2009)

The year-old kitten
has never seen snow,
fallen or falling, until now
this late winter afternoon.

He sits with wide eyes
at the firelit window, sees
white things falling
from black trees.

Are they petals, leaves or birds?
They cannot be the cabbage whites
he batted briefly with his paws,
or the puffball seeds in summer grass...

'Where do they go?' he questions,
with eyes ablaze, following their flight
into black stone. So I put him
out into the yard, to make their acquaintance.

He has to look up at them: when one
blanches his coral nose, he sneezes,
and flicks a few from his whiskers, from
his sharpened ear, that picks up silences.

He catches one on a curled-up paw
and licks it quickly, before
its strange milk fades, then sniffs its ghost,
a wetness, while his black coat

shivers with stars of flickering frost.
— And with something else that makes his thin
tail swish, his fur on end!
Then he suddenly scoots in

and sits again with wide eyes
at the firelit window, sees
white things falling
from black trees.

From *The Kitten and the Falling Leaves*
WILLIAM WORDSWORTH (1770—1850)

... See, the Kitten on the Wall,
Sporting with the leaves that fall.
Wither'd leaves, one, two, and three
from the lofty Elder-tree! ...
Each invisible and mute,
in his wavering parachute.
But the Kitten, how she starts,
– Crouches, stretches, paws, and darts!
First at one and then its fellow,
Just as light and just as yellow;
There are many now – now one –
Now they stop; and there are none –
What intenseness of desire
In her upward eye of fire!
With a tiger-leap half way,
Now she meets the coming prey,
Lets it go as fast, and then
Has it in her power again:
Now she works with three or four,
Like an Indian Conjuror;
Quick as he in feats of art,
Far beyond in joy of heart.
Were her antics play'd in the eye

Of a thousand Standers-by,
Clapping hands with shout and stare,
What would little Tabby care!
For the plaudits of the Crowd?
Over happy to be proud,
over wealthy in the treasure
Of her own exceeding pleasure!

To Coney: My Kitten
(A Poem under Difficulties)
ELEANOR FARJEON (1881—1965)

Kitten like a ball of gold,
Not much more than ten weeks old,
Must you really try to bite
My penholder as I write?
Must you really cut up capers
All along my notes and papers?
Must you really, do you think,
Dip your tail into my ink
And on my tale wipe it dry?
Do you really have to try
Making a duet of it
While I type-write, golden kit?
Kitten! that's my pencil, please!

Kitten! those are my two knees!
Kitten! why by all the laws,
Have you pins instead of claws?
Kitten! I am not a tree —
Don't come clambering up me!
Go away, you little blighter!
You're a kitten, I'm a writer,
And if you my verses chew,
How can I buy milk for you?
Did you hear me? Go away! …

Oh, all right, then. Stay and play.

Familiarity Dangerous
WILLIAM COWPER (1731—1800)

As in her ancient mistress' lap,
The youthful tabby lay,
They gave each other many a tap,
Alike dispos'd to play.
But strife ensues. Puss waxes warm
And with protruded claws
Ploughs all the length of Lydia's arm,
Mere wantonness the cause.
At once, resentful of the deed,

She shakes her to the ground
With many a threat that she shall bleed
With still a deeper wound.
But, Lydia, bid thy fury rest!
It was a venial stroke;
For she that will with kittens jest,
Should bear a kitten's joke!

Translated from a Latin poem
by Vincent Bourne (1695—1747)

Foreign Kittens
OLIVER HERFORD (1863—1935)

Kittens large and Kittens small,
Prowling on the Back Yard Wall,
Though your fur be rough and few,
I should like to play with you.
Though you roam the dangerous street,
And have curious things to eat,
Though you sleep in barn or loft,
With no cushions warm and soft,
Though you have to stay out-of-doors
When it's cold or when it pours,
Though your fur is all askew —
How I'd like to play with you!

From *Old Tom-cat into Damsel Gay*

PAUL SCARRON (1610–1660)

...This Lady had a Cat whom she
Adored quite immoderately;
For his amusement once, her whim
Invented a disguise for him...
A fine, white, laundered linen shirt
A little jacket and a skirt,
A collar and a neckerchief
Made, with the help of her belief,
Old Tom-cat into Damsel gay...
Whatever happened then took place
Because she failed to embrace
Her Cat as closely as she might.
Without considering wrong or right,
The good Cat gained the stair,
And then the attic, and from there
Out upon the tiles he strayed;
Loudly crying, the Lady prayed
Her servants instantly to be
Out after him assiduously:

But in the country of the tiles
Wary Tom-cats show their wiles.
They searched for him until they tired,

And the next day they inquired
Of the neighbours...
And all the while the Cat uncaged
Never returned; the Lady raged
Less for her necklace's expense
Than for her Tom-cat vanished thence.

A Cat

EDWARD THOMAS (1878–1917)

She had a name among the children:
But no one loved though someone owned
Her, locked her out of doors at bedtime
And had her kittens duly drowned.

In Spring, nevertheless, this cat
Ate blackbirds, thrushes, nightingales,
And birds of bright voice, and plume, and flight,
As well as scraps from neighbours' pails.

I loathed and hated her for this;
One speckle on a thrush's breast
Was worth a million such: and yet
She lived long, till God gave her rest.

From *On the Death of a Favourite Cat,*
Drowned in a Tub of Gold Fishes
THOMAS GRAY (1716–1771)

'Twas on a lofty vase's side,
Where China's gayest art had dy'd
   The azure flowers that blow,
Demurest of the tabby kind,
The pensive Selima, reclin'd,
   Gaz'd on the lake below.

Her conscious tail her joy declar'd;
The fair round face, the snowy beard,
   The velvet of her paws,
Her coat, that with the tortoise vies,
Her ears of jet, and emerald eyes,
   She saw; and purr'd applause.

Still had she gaz'd; but 'midst the tide
Two angel forms were seen to glide,
   The Genii of the stream:
Their scaly armour's Tyrian hue
Thro' richest purple to the view
   Betray'd a golden gleam...

Presumptuous Maid! with looks intent
Again she stretch'd, again she bent,
    Nor knew the gulf between.
(Malignant Fate sat by, and smil'd)
The slipp'ry verge her feet beguil'd,
    She tumbled headlong in.

Eight times emerging from the flood
She mew'd to ev'ry wat'ry God,
    Some speedy aid to send.
No dolphin came, no nereid stirr'd;
Nor cruel Tom, nor Susan heard.
    A Fav'rite has no friend!

From hence, ye Beauties undeceiv'd,
Know, one false step is ne'er retriev'd,
    And be with caution bold.
Not all that tempts your wand'ring eyes
And heedless hearts is lawful prize;
    Nor all that glisters, gold.

From the Prologue to
The Wife of Bath's Tale
GEOFFREY CHAUCER (1343–1400)

The cat, if you but singe her tabby skin,
The chimney keeps, and sits content within:
But once grown sleek, will from the corner run,
Sport with her tail and wanton in the sun:
She licks her fair round face and frisks abroad
To show her fur, and to be catterwaw'd.'

From *The Canterbury Tales*,
translated by Alexander Pope

From *Verses on a Cat*
PERCY BYSSHE SHELLEY (1792–1822)

A cat in distress,
Nothing more, nor less;
Good folks, I must faithfully tell ye,
As I am a sinner,
It waits for some dinner
To stuff out its own little belly.

You would not easily guess
    All the modes of distress
Which torture the tenants of earth;
    And the various evils,
    Which like so many devils,
Attend the poor souls from their birth...

    One wants society,
    Another variety,
Others a tranquil life;
    Some want food,
    Others, as good,
Only want a wife.

    But this poor little cat
    Only wanted a rat,
To stuff out its own little maw;
    And it were as good
    Some people had such food,
To make them hold their jaw!

Had Tiberius Been a Cat
MATTHEW ARNOLD (1822–1888)

– Cruel, but composed and bland,
Dumb, inscrutable and grand,
So Tiberius might have sat,
Had Tiberius been a cat.

From *Poor Matthias A Downy Cove*
ANON

A downy cove is our old tom-cat,
Just turned thirty years old;
He eateth the lean, and leaveth the fat
And won't touch his meals when too cold.
His food must be crumbled, and not decayed,
To pleasure his dainty whim,
But a turkey-bone from the kitchen-maid
Is a very good meal for him.

From *The Rat-Catcher and Rats*
JOHN GAY (1685–1732)

The rats by night such mischief did,
Betty was every morning chid:
They undermined whole sides of bacon,
Her cheese was sapped, her tarts were taken...
She cursed the Cat, for want of duty.
Who left her foes a constant booty.
An engineer, of noted skill,
Engaged to stop the growing ill.
From room to room he now surveys
Their haunts, their works, their secret ways...
And envious Cat from place to place
Unseen, attends his silent pace:
She saw that, if his trade went on,
The purring race must be undone;
So secretly removes his baits,
And every strategem defeats...
Incensed, he cries, 'This very hour
The wretch shall bleed beneath my power.'
So said, a ponderous trap he brought,
And in the fact poor Puss was caught...
The captive Cat, with piteous mews,
For pardon, life, and freedom sues.
'A sister of the science spare;

One interest is our common care.'
'What insolence!' the man replied;
'Shall cats with us the game divide?
Were all your interloping band
Extinguished, or expelled the land,
We Rat-catchers might raise our fees,
Sole guardians of a nation's cheese!'
A Cat, who saw the lifted knife,
Thus spoke, and saved her sister's life.
'In every age and clime we see,
Two of a trade can ne'er agree.
Each hates his neighbour for encroaching:
Squire stigmatizes squire for poaching...
But let us limit our desires,
Not war like beauties, kings, and squires;
For though we both one prey pursue,
There's game enough for us and you.'

A Cat's Conscience
ANON

A Dog will often steal a bone,
But conscience lets him not alone,
And by his tail his guilt is known.

But cats consider theft a game,
And, howsoever you may blame,
Refuse the slightest sign of shame.

When food mysteriously goes,
The chances are that Pussy knows
More than she leads you to suppose.

And hence there is no need for you
If Pussy declines a meal or two,
To feel her pulse and make ado.

From *The Retired Cat*

WILLIAM COWPER (1731–1800)

A poet's cat, sedate and grave,
As poet well could wish to have,
Was much addicted to inquire
For nooks, to which she might retire,
And where, secure as mouse in chink,
She might repose, or sit and think...

A drawer – it chanc'd, at bottom lin'd
With linen of the softest kind,
With such as merchants introduce
From India, for the ladies' use –
A draw'r impending o'er the rest,
Half open in the topmost chest,
Of depth enough, and none to spare,
Invited her to slumber there.
Puss with delight beyond expression,
Survey'd the scene, and took possession.
Recumbent at her ease ere long,
And lull'd by her own hum-drum song,
She left the cares of life behind,
And slept as she would sleep her last,
When in came, housewifely inclin'd,
The chambermaid, and shut it fast;

By no malignity impell'd,
But all unconscious whom it held.

Awaken'd by the shock, cried Puss,
'Was ever cat attended thus!
The open draw'r was left, I see,
Merely to prove a nest for me,
For soon as I was well compos'd,
Then came the maid, and it was clos'd.
How smooth these 'kerchiefs, and how sweet,
Oh, what a delicate retreat!
I will resign myself to rest
Till Sol, declining in the west,
Shall call to supper; when, no doubt,
Susan will come and let me out.'

The evening came, the sun descended,
And Puss remain'd still unattended.
The night roll'd tardily away,
(With her indeed 'twas never day)
The sprightly morn her course renew'd,
The evening grey again ensued,
And Puss came into mind no more
Than if entomb'd the day before.
With hunger pinch'd, and pinch'd for room,
She now presag'd approaching doom,

Nor slept a single wink, or purr'd,
Conscious of jeopardy incurr'd.

That night, by chance, the poet watching,
Heard an inexplicable scratching,
His noble heart went pit-a-pat
And to himself he said — what's that?...
At length a voice which well he knew,
A long and melancholy mew,
Saluting his poetic ears,
Consol'd him, and dispell'd his fears;
He left his bed, he trod the floor,
He 'gan in haste the draw'rs explore,
The lowest first, and without stop,
The rest in order to the top.
For 'tis a truth well known to most,
That whatsoever thing is lost,
We seek it, ere it come to light,
In ev'ry cranny but the right.
Forth skipp'd the cat; not now replete
As erst with airy self-conceit,
Nor in her own fond apprehension
A theme for all the world's attention,
But modest, sober, cur'd of all
Her notions hyperbolical,
And wishing for a place of rest

Anything rather than a chest
Then stepp'd the poet into bed,
With this reflection in his head:
    MORAL
Beware of too sublime a sense
Of your own worth and consequence...

From *Sad Memories*
CHARLES STUART CALVERLEY (1831–1884)

They tell me I am beautiful: they praise my silken
    hair,
My little feet that silently slip on from stair to
    stair:
They praise my pretty trustful face and innocent
    grey eye;
Fond hands caress me oftentimes, yet would that I
    might die!
Why was I born to be abhorred of man and bird
    and beast?
The bulfinch marks me stealing by, and straight his
    song hath ceased;
The shrewmouse eyes me shudderingly, then flees;
    and, worse than that,

The housedog he flees after me — why was I born a
   cat?...
'I remember, I remember,' how one night I 'fleeted
   by',
And gain'd the blessed tiles and gazed into the
   cold clear sky.
'I remember, I remember, how my little lovers
   came;'
And there, beneath the crescent moon,
   played many a little game.
They fought — by good St. Catharine, 'twas
   a fearsome sight to see
The coal-black crest, the glowering orbs, of one
   gigantic He.
Like bow by some tall bowman bent at Hastings
   or Poitiers,
His huge back curved, till none observed a vestige
   of his ears:
He stood, an ebon crescent, flouting that ivory
   moon;
Then raised the pibroch of his race, the Song
   without a Tune;
Gleam'd his white teeth, his mammoth tail waved
   darkly to and fro,
As with one complex yell he burst, all claws,
   upon the foe.

It thrills me now, that final Miaow — that weird
  unearthly din:
Lone maidens heard it far away, and leaped out of
  their skin.
A potboy from his den o'erhead peep'd with a
  scared wan face;
Then sent a random brickbat down, which
  knocked me into space.
Nine days I fell, or thereabouts: and, had we not
  nine lives,
I wish I ne'er had seen again thy sausage-shop,
  St. Ives!
Had I, as some cats have, nine tails, how gladly
  I would lick
The hand, and person generally, of him who
  heaved that brick!
For me they fill the milkbowl up, and cull the
  choice sardine:
But ah! I nevermore shall be the cat I once have
  been!
The memories of that fatal night they haunt me
  even now:
In dreams I see that rampant He, and tremble
  at that Miaow.

Pussy Can Sit by the Fire
RUDYARD KIPLING (1865–1936)

Pussy can sit by the fire and sing,
Pussy can climb a tree
Or play with a silly old cork and string
To 'muse herself, not me.
But I like Binkie my dog, because
He knows how to behave;
So, Binkie's the same as the First Friend was,
And I am the Man in the Cave!
Pussy will play Man Friday till
It's time to wet her paw
and make her walk on the window-sill
(For the footprint Crusoe saw);
Then she fluffles her tail and mews,
And scratches and won't attend
But Binkie will play whatever I choose,
And he is my true First Friend!
Pussy will rub my knees with her head
Pretending she loves me hard;
But the very minute I go to my bed
Pussy runs out in the yard,
And there she stays till the morning-light;
So I know it is only pretend
And he is my Firstest Friend.

The Dog
OLIVER HERFORD (1863–1935)

The Dog is black or white or brown
    And sometimes spotted like a clown.
He loves to make a foolish noise
    And Human Company enjoys.

The Human People pat his head
    And teach him to pretend he's dead,
And beg, and fetch and carry too;
    Things that no well-bred Cat will do.

At Human jokes, however stale.
    He jumps about and wags his tail,
And Human People clap their hands
    And think he really understands.

They say 'Good Dog' to him. To us
    They say 'Poor Puss' and make no fuss.
Why Dogs are 'good' and Cats are 'poor'
    I fail to understand, I'm sure.

To Someone very Good and Just,
    Who has proved worthy of her trust,
A Cat will sometimes condescend –
    The Dog is Everybody's friend.

False Kindness
ANON

The softest little fluff of fur!
The gentlest, most persuasive purr!
Oh, everybody told me that
She was the loveliest little cat...
Of course I spoiled her. When she sprung
Upon the table when quite young
I only put her gently down
And said 'No, no!' and tried to frown.

Now, large and quick, and strong of will
She springs upon the table still;
In spite of my most watchful care
She steals the food which tempts her there.
But I acknowledge with much shame
That it is I who am to blame;
When she was young, had I been kind,
I would have made my kitten mind.

From *On Lutestrings Catt-Eaten*

THOMAS MASTER (1603—1643)

...Could these neglected shreads you see
Inspire a Lute of Ivorie
And make it speake? Oh! think then what
Hath beene committed by my catt,
Who in the silence of this night
Hath gnawne these cords, and marr'd them quite;
Leaving such reliques as may be
For fretts, not for my lute but me.
Pusse, I will curse thee; may'st thou dwell
With some dry Hermit in a cell
Where Ratt neere peep'd, where mouse neere fedd,
And flyes goes supperlesse to bedd;
Or with some close-par'd Brother, where
Thou'lt fast each Sabbath in the yeare;
Or else, prophane, be hang'd on Munday,
For butchering a mouse on Sunday;
Or May'st thou tumble from some tower,
And misse to light upon fower,
Taking a fall that may untie
Eight of nine lives, and let them flye;
Or may the midnight embers sindge
Thy daintie coate, or Jane beswinge
Thy hide, when she shall take thee biting

Her cheese clouts, or her house beshiting.
What, was there neere a ratt nor mouse,
Nor Buttery ope? nought in the house
But harmlesse Lutestrings could suffice
Thy paunch, and draw thy glaring eyes?...
    Thus, pusse, thou seest what might betyde thee;
But I forebeare to hurt or chide thee;
For may be pusse was melancholy
And so to make her blythe and jolly,
Finding these strings, shee'ld have a fitt
Of mirth; nay, pusse, if that were it,
Thus I revenge mee, that as thou
Hast played on them, I've plaid on you;
And as thy touche was nothing fine,
Soe I've but scratch'd these notes of mine.

A Modest Cat's Soliloquy
ANON

Far down within the damp, dark earth
The grimy miner goes
That I on chilly nights may have
A fire to warm my toes;
Brave sailors plough through the wintry main
Through peril and mishap,

46

That I, on Oriental rugs,
May take my morning nap.
Out in the distant meadow
Meekly graze the lowing kine
That milk in endless saucerfuls
All foaming, may be mine;
The fish that swim the ocean
And the birds that fill the air —
Did I not like to pick their bones,
Pray, think you they'd be there?

K was a Kitten
ANON

K was a Kitten,
Who'd jump at a cork,
And learn'd to eat mice
Without plate, knife or fork.

And L was a Lady,
Who made him so wise
But he tore her long train,
And she cried out her eyes.

From the *Alphabet of Goody Two Shoes* (1808)

To a Cat

HARTLEY COLERIDGE (1796–1849)

Nellie, methinks, 'twixt thee and me
There is a kind of sympathy;
And could we interchange our nature –
If I were cat, thou human creature –
I should, like thee, be no great mouser,
And thou, like me, no great composer;
For, like thy plaintive mews, my muse
With villainous whine doth fate abuse,
Because it hath not made me sleek
As golden down on Cupid's cheek;
And yet thou canst upon the rug lie,
Stretch'd out like snail, or curled up snugly,
As if thou wert not lean or ugly;
And I, who in poetic flights
Sometimes complain of sleepless nights,
Regardless of the sun in heaven,
Am apt to doze till past eleven –
The world would just the same go round
If I were hanged and thou wert drowned;
There is one difference, 'tis true:
Thou dost not know it, and I do.

Mr Sheraton's Cat
ELEANOR FARJEON (1881–1965)

Mr Sheraton had a cat,
I'm certain of that.

Mr Sheraton's cat's
Pats
Posed so prettily on the floor –
Two behind and two before,
While Puss herself demurely stood
Graceful, proportioned, perfect, good –
That Mr Sheraton eyeing the sweet
Turn of those small fastidious feet,
Cried: 'Eureka! At last I'm able
To turn the legs of my chair and table!'
Men praised his work then and thereafter.

The feline race subdues its laughter,
And gazes down its exquisite legs
To its turned out pads that can walk on eggs,
Purrs: 'Mr Sheraton's credit? That's
Mr Sheraton's cat's.'

From *The Song of Kruger the Cat*
CHARLES CAUSLEY (1917–2003)

I really hate the coal-man.
I hate his hood and sack.
I'm sure one day he'll carry me off
In a bundle on his back.

When he crunches up to the bunker
And I hear the coal go crump
My legs turn into custard
And my heart begins to bump.

I'm not afraid of a bulldog,
A gull or giant rat,
The milkman or the postman,
Or the plumber, come to that.

But when I hear the coal-man
I shake and quake with fright.
And I'm up and away for the rest of the day
And sometimes half the night...

'Now Kruger dear,' they say, 'look here:
Isn't it rather droll?
You love to sleep and snore before
A fire that's made of coal.'

But I can't help my feelings
However hard I try.
I really hate the coal-man
Who's that? Good grief! Goodbye!

Cats' Meat
ANON

You, who've rejected the pick of the dish
And flatly refuse to be stirred
By the mention of meat if you know there is fish
Or of fish if you know there is bird.
Who insist on your sole being a la bonne femme
And your chicken direct from the breast
Who will only touch trout that has recently come
From the shadowy shoals of the Test,
You who drink nothing that isn't Grade A
And would turn up your nose at a mouse,
Whom I've actually seen moving coldly away
From an underhung portion of grouse,
You who will listlessly trifle and toy
With a dream of a cod kedgeree
Are eating with every appearance of joy
    A very decayed bumble bee.

The Owl and the Pussycat
EDWARD LEAR (1812–1888)

The Owl and the Pussy-Cat went to sea
    In a beautiful pea-green boat,
They took some honey, and plenty of money,
    Wrapped up in a five-pound note.
The Owl looked up to the stars above,
    And sang to a small guitar,
'O lovely Pussy! O Pussy my love,
    What a beautiful Pussy you are,
        You are,
        You are!
What a beautiful Pussy you are!'

Pussy said to the Owl, 'You elegant fowl!
    How charmingly sweet you sing!
O let us be married! too long we have tarried:
    But what shall we do for a ring?'
They sailed away, for a year and a day,
    To the land where the Bong-tree grows
And there in a wood a Piggy-wig stood
    With a ring at the end of his nose,
        His nose,
        His nose,
With a ring at the end of his nose.

'Dear pig, are you willing to sell for one shilling
    Your ring?' Said the Piggy, 'I will.'
So they took it away, and were married next day
    By the Turkey who lives on the hill.
They dined on mince, and slices of quince,
    Which they ate with a runcible spoon;
And hand in hand, on the edge of the sand,
    They danced by the light of the moon,
        The moon,
        The moon,
They danced by the light of the moon.

The Shadow Kitten
OLIVER HERFORD (1863–1935)

There's a funny little kitten that tries to look
    like me,
But, though I'm round and fluffy, he's as flat as flat
    can be;
And when I try to mew to him he never makes
    a sound,
And when I jump into the air he never leaves
    the ground.

53

He has a way of growling I don't understand at all.
Sometimes he's very little and sometimes he's
  very tall.
And once when in the garden when the sun came
  up at dawn
He grew so big I think he stretched half-way across
  the lawn.

Milk for the Cat
HAROLD MONRO (1879–1932)

When the tea is brought at five o'clock,
And all the neat curtains are drawn with care,
The little black cat with bright green eyes
Is suddenly purring there.

At first she pretends, having nothing to do,
She has come in merely to blink by the grate,
But, though tea may be late or the milk may be sour,
She is never late.

And presently her agate eyes
Take a soft large milky haze,
And her independent casual glance
Becomes a stiff, hard gaze.

Then she stamps her claws or lifts her ears,
Or twists her tail and begins to stir,
Till suddenly all her lithe body becomes
One breathing, trembling purr.

The children eat and wriggle and laugh;
The two old ladies stroke their silk:
But the cat is grown small and thin with desire,
Transformed to a creeping lust for milk.

The white saucer like some full moon descends
At last from the clouds of the table above;
She sighs and dreams and thrills and glows,
Transfigured with love.

She nestles over the shining rim,
Buries her chin in the creamy sea;
Her tail hangs loose; each drowsy paw
Is doubled under each bending knee.

A long, dim ecstasy holds her life;
Her world is an infinite shapeless white,
Till her tongue has curled the last holy drop,
Then she sinks back into the night,

Draws and dips her body to heap
Her sleepy nerves in the great arm-chair,
Lies defeated and buried deep
Three or four hours unconscious there.

I Had a Little Cat
CHARLES CAUSLEY (1917–2003)

I had a little cat called Tim Tom Tay
I took him to town on market day,
I combed his whiskers, I brushed his tail,
I wrote on a label 'Cat for Sale.
Knows how to deal with rats and mice.
Two pounds fifty. Bargain price.'

But when the people came to buy
I saw such a look in Tim Tom's eye
That it was clear as clear could be
I couldn't sell Tim for a fortune's fee.
I was shamed and sorry, I'll tell you plain
And I took home Tim Tom Tay again.

From *To a Cat*

ALGERNON CHARLES SWINBURNE
(1837–1909)

Stately, kindly, lordly friend,
   Condescend
Here to sit by me, and turn
Glorious eyes that smile and burn,
Golden eyes, love's lustrous meed,
On the golden page I read.

All your wondrous wealth of hair,
   Dark and fair,
Silken-shaggy, soft and bright
As the clouds and beams of night,
Pays my reverent hand's caress
Back with friendlier gentleness.

Dogs may fawn on all and some
   As they come;
You, a friend of loftier mind,
Answer friends alone in kind;
Just your foot upon my hand
Softly bids it understand...

Wild on woodland ways your sires
    Flashed like fires;
Fair as flame and fierce and fleet
As with wings on wingless feet
Shone and sprang your mother, free,
Bright and brave as wind or sea.

Free and proud and glad as they,
    Here to-day
Rests or roams their radiant child,
Vanquished not, but reconciled,
Free from curb of aught above
Save the lovely curb of love...

Pussy
ANON (c. 1830)

I like little pussy, her coat is so warm;
And if I don't hurt her, she'll do me no harm.
So I'll not pull her tail, nor drive her away,
But pussy and I very gently will play.
She shall sit by my side, and I'll give her some
    food;
And she'll love me because I am gentle and good.

I'll pat pretty pussy, and then she will purr;
And thus show her thanks for my kindness to her.
But I'll not pinch her ears, nor tread on her paw,
Lest I should provoke her to use her sharp claw.
I never will vex her, nor make her displeased –
For pussy don't like to be worried or teased.

Le Chat Noir

GRAHAM TOMSON (1863–1911)

Half loving-kindliness, and half disdain,
Thou comest to my call, serenely suave,
With humming speech and gracious gesture grave,
In salutation courtly and urbane.
Yet must I humble me thy grace to gain,
For wiles may win thee, but no arts enslave,
And nowhere gladly thou abidest, save
Where naught disturbs the concord of thy reign.
Sphinx of my quiet hearth! who deignst to dwell
Friend of my toil, companion of mine ease,
Thine is the lore of Ra and Rameses;
That men forget dost thou remember well,
Beholden still in blinking reveries,
With sombre, sea-green gaze inscrutable.

On Mrs Reynolds's Cat
JOHN KEATS (1795–1821)

Cat! who hast pass'd thy grand climacteric,
   How many mice and rats hast in thy days
   Destroy'd? – How many tit bits stolen? Gaze
With those bright languid segments green, and
   prick
Those velvet ears – but pr'ythee do not stick
   Thy latent talons in me – and upraise
   Thy gentle mew – and tell me all thy frays
Of fish and mice, and rats and tender chick.
Nay, look not down, nor lick thy dainty wrists –
   For all the wheezy asthma, – and for all
Thy tail's tip is nick'd off – and though the fists
   Of many a maid have given thee many a maul,
Still is that fur as soft as when the lists
   In youth thou enter'dst on glass bottled wall.

From *The Cat*
LYTTON STRACHEY (1880–1932)

Dear creature by the fire a-purr,
   Strange idol, eminently bland,
Miraculous puss! As o'er your fur

I trail a negligible hand,
And gaze into your gazing eyes,
    And wonder in a demi-dream,
What mystery it is that lies,
    Behind those slits that glare and gleam,
An exquisite enchantment falls...
    An ampler air, a warmer June
    Enfold me, and my wondering eye
Salutes a more imperial moon
    Throned in a more resplendent sky
Than ever knew this northern shore.
    Oh, strange! For you are with me, too,
And I who am a cat once more
    Follow the woman that was you
With tail erect and pompous march,
    The proudest puss that ever trod,
Through many a grove, 'neath many an arch,
    Impenetrable as a god.
Down many an alabaster flight
    Of broad and cedar-shaded stairs,
While over us the elaborate night
    Mysteriously gleams and glares.

From *The Sphinx*

Oscar Wilde (1854–1900)

In a dim corner of my room for longer than my
    fancy thinks,
A beautiful and silent Sphinx has watched me
    through the shifting gloom.

Inviolate and immobile she does not rise,
    she does not stir
For silver moons are naught to her and
    naught to her the suns that reel...

Dawn follows Dawn and Nights grow old
    and all the while this curious cat
Lies crouching on the Chinese mat with eyes of
    satin rimmed with gold...

Come forth my lovely languorous Sphinx!
    and put your head upon my knee!
And let me stroke your throat and see your body
    spotted like the Lynx!

And let me touch those curving claws of
    yellow ivory, and grasp
The tail that like a monstrous Asp coils round
    your heavy velvet paws!...

The Cats
CHARLES BAUDELAIRE (1821–1867)

The lover and the stern philosopher
Both love, in their ripe time, the confident
Soft cats, the house's chiefest ornament,
Who like themselves are cold and seldom stir.

Of knowledge and of pleasures amorous,
Silence they seek and Darkness' fell domain;
Had not their proud souls scorned to brook
   his rein,
They would have made grim steed for Erebus.

Pensive they rest in noble attitudes
Like great stretched sphinxes in vast solitudes
Which seem to sleep wrapt in an endless dream;

Their fruitful loins are full of sparks divine,
And gleams of gold within their pupils shine
As 'twere within the shadow of a stream.

Translated by Jack Collings Squire, 1909

The Cat
ANON

You see the beauty of the world
Through eyes of unalloyed content,
And in my study chair upcurled,
Move me to pensive wonderment.

I wish I knew your trick of thought,
The perfect balance of your ways:
They seem an inspiration, caught
From other laws in older days.

This Old Cat
K.C. SIEVERT BINGAMON

For Misty-Dawn
I'm getting on in years,
My coat is turning gray.
My eyes have lost their luster,
My hearing... just okay.
I spend my whole day dreaming
Of conquests in my past,
Lying near a sunny window,
Waiting for its warm repast.

I remember our first visit,
I was coming to you free,
Hoping you would take me in
And keep me company.
I wasn't young or handsome,
Two years I'd roamed the street,
There were scars upon my face,
I hobbled on my feet.

I could sense your disappointment
As I left my prison cage.
Oh, I hoped you would accept me
And look beyond my age.
You took me out of pity,
I accepted without shame.
Then you grew to love me,
And I admit the same.

I have shared with you your laughter,
You have wet my fur with tears.
We've come to know each other
Throughout these many years.
Just ONE more hug this morning
Before you drive away,
And know I'll think about you
Throughout your busy day!

The time we've left together
Is a treasured time at that.
My heart is yours forever, I promise
This Old Cat.

An Epitaph
ANON

'Tis false that all of pussy's race
Regard not person but the place,
For here lies one who, could she tell
Her stories by some magic spell,
Would, from the quitted barn and grove,
Her sporting haunts, to show her love,
At sound of footsteps, absent long,
Of those she soothed with purring song,
Leap to their arms in fond embrace,
For love of them, and not for place.

From the tombstone of a cat, Meaford Hall,
near Stone, Staffordshire

On the Death of a Cat,
a Friend of Mine, Aged Ten Years
and a Half

CHRISTINA ROSSETTI (1830—1894)

Who shall tell the lady's grief
When her Cat was past relief?
Who shall number the hot tears
Shed o'er her, beloved for years?
Who shall say the dark dismay
Which her dying caused that day?

Come, ye Muses, one and all,
Come obedient to my call;
Come and mourn, with tuneful breath
Each one for a separate death;
And while you in numbers sigh,
I will sing her elegy.

Of a noble race she came,
And Grimalkin was her name
Young and old full many a mouse
Felt the prowess of her house:

Weak and strong full many a rat
Cowered beneath her crushing pat:
And the birds around the place
Shrank from her too close embrace.

But one night, reft of her strength,
She lay down and died at length:
Lay a kitten by her side,
In whose life the mother died.
Spare her line and lineage,
Guard her kitten's tender age,
And that kitten's name as wide
Shall be known as hers that died.

And whoever passes by
The poor grave where Puss doth lie,
Softly, softly let him tread,
Nor disturb her narrow bed.

Last Words to a Dumb Friend
THOMAS HARDY (1840–1928)

Pet was never mourned as you
Purrer of the spotless hue,
Plumy tail, and wistful gaze
While you humoured our queer ways,
Or outshrilled your morning call
Up the stairs and through the hall –
Foot suspended in its fall –
While, expectant, you would stand
Arched to meet the stroking hand;
Till your way you chose to wend
Yonder, to your tragic end.

Never another pet for me!
Let your place all vacant be;
Better blankness day by day
Than companion torn away.
Better bid his memory fade,
Better blot each mark he made,
Selfishly escape distress
By contrived forgetfulness,
Than preserve his prints to make
Every morn and eve an ache.

From the chair whereon he sat
Sweep his fur, nor wince thereat;
Rake his little pathways out
Mid the bushes roundabout;
Smooth away his talons' mark
From the claw-worn pine-tree bark,
Where he climbed as dusk embrowned,
Waiting us who loitered round...

Housemate, I can think you still
Bounding to the window-sill,
Over which I vaguely see
Your small mound beneath the tree,
Showing in the autumn shade
That you moulder where you played.